SPJ

Tom Jenks

Published by   BLART BOOKS

www.blartmagazine.jimdo.com

ISBN 978-1-326-40868-8

Sections of this poem appeared in issue 31 of The Wolf and in issue 4 of Three And A Half Point 9. Thanks to the editors.

do not eat the berries by the Build A Bear Workshop
the berries by the Build A Bear Workshop are poisonous
no make-up selfie in the clearance aisle

a stag glimpsed amongst the coleslaw
in the overspill car park where the shamans are
salmon in the standing pools

I will meet you by the memorial bush
I will meet you on the sacred mound
got an amulet and a rotisserie chicken

the weight of the potato before it is cooked

the weight of the potato after it is cooked

the weight of the world in mirrored water

in a magical mirror her occult third eyebrow

on the back of a spoon in a chemical toilet

once more the emperor slips into slumber

back at the Gatsby themed Tupperware party

when I was spammed by a future world champion

in a mobile library on the shores of a loch

summer evening winter evening winter fox silver bear

mail order chain mail apprentice mosquitoes

six tree surgeons from the former Westmoreland

slow lights in the tender grass

in the maize maze sudden stench of pickle

not how you dreamt it smell of a steak bake

they are selling marine flares in Asda George

there are spectres there one size too small

in the lair of the lions where the sushi is

the incredible story of a truly brave pigeon
in congress by the tower of mincemeat
meteors above the designer outlet

in a walk-in larder the sacred herbs
the Yorkshire terriers will guide you home
down the green lanes in the year of the stoat

two arcs on linoleum partially intersecting
like ley lines at the organic cheesemonger
like a fun fight at the fondue factory

an unhatched egg at Gulliver's World
Piers Morgan refers obliquely to Lenin
buttered bagels at the mausoleum

a lukewarm peach at the webinar
six bulbs blazing one extinguished
yellow leaves green leaves white vinegar red salt

muted kerfuffle in the arboretum
a marital aid in the druid's copse
they found a solution to the monkey puzzle trees

in the halls of St. Luke a garden suburb
a bird flew through and was noted in the minutes
leakage from headphones in industrial units

redolent blossom a cache of brie
bags of charcoal in sheltered housing
yellow hoods at the business park

on her birthday with champagne grapefruit
in a dream she obstructed the driver's door
scrambled egg on the family crest

sleek on leopard print an infomercial

rampant bullfinch rendered metaphorically

in the lobby the imponderable owls

a shaft of air surrounds you Mabel

here in the greenwood with a gastric band

down the log flume the ancient frigate

in the evening we have scant reception

sunken precincts of the lost domain

England through the casement green and miniature

on a narrow boat holiday with the cast of *Hollyoaks*
we are communists now we share the shower gel
eggs benedict and soufflé Monte Cristo

herons high above the Travelodge
the vanished wash bag of Raymond Queneau
a stack of unordered pink marshmallows

drone of abandoned mobility scooters
somewhere beneath the dome of the forest
out there immaculate the sarcasm of rooks

got his top off on his LinkedIn profile

at the Challenge Cup final they are all wearing towels

in the long long gardens repeating rhododendrons

I am battling daemons my addiction to salami

at the leisure centre with the shaolin monks

in the soft play area with the IBS sufferers

I'd like an office in the palm of my hand

what are some things that fool people all the time

what are the most mind-blowing facts about Switzerland

dance off at the pop up podiatrist

six blue mink in the municipal treehouse

an array of poodles grandly named

clipped close and lost in the laurel maze

got a letter printed in *Take A Break*

badly dubbed at the water cooler

in an unseen episode of *Eldorado*

he is in the wine bar in linen slacks

at the salon with a bucket of quiche

slightly foxed by a particular nook

I was writing the ransom notes out in longhand

in the vestibule an implacable bullock

a flash mob of disgruntled accountants

by the partially functioning mini roundabout

bird cloud as the birds ascend

there amongst the bottled plums

with an antelope that triggers the sensors

with a lo-cal tiramisu you will find me

a rare reversal in the European leg

we collaborated and lost 18 lbs.

we ran the numbers through the abacus

her face reflected twice in the mill pond

an area manager commands the dragons

in nylon sportswear with lemon piping

you know where you are with buffalo wings

hickory nuts enjoyed in the priest hole

£1 brunch every day in the mead hall

a dream of being baffled by bears
in the underground chambers of the sorting office
starlight in the Hot Yoga Taster

I like it when she folds up the blanket
in a pocket of shade by the sausage concession
in a small copse in the metropolitan borough

like a nectarine dropped in a wishing well
like tapas on a replacement bus
like a waistcoat at the otter sanctuary

down the bridleway in a baseball cap

England where the pine cones fall

a rubber of whist with Clement Attlee

the paisley cravat of Larry Grayson

the burgundy slacks of Jerry Leadbetter

early closing at the umbrella museum

John Barrowman explains how to x-ray a snake

Nick Hewer talks to Deborah Meaden about rhinos

it is morning once again in Altrincham

out in the shaded acres with Raunce

dark green apples under the limes

a ripple across the ornamental pond

a concealed prism dazzles the peacocks

the quiet invention of the pomegranate

the sugar cubes in the sugar bowls

grooves down which the bearings run

this clock made of clocks is the coolest thing

my nephew's phone puts yellow squares on faces

a cormorant destroyed the prize winning model

shrubbery exceeding the maximum height

behind the authentic replica yurt

the secret turmoil of Jason Orange

pollock fingers and garlic cheese rope

through the sycamores the Avon representative

a sapling shaded by taller saplings

here the great plague came ashore

and spread via hummus in communal fridges

abashed in the deer park the turbulent priest

asleep on the luxury walnut grab bags

a petition to quell the chitchat of choughs

great system analysts are born not made

at the mixologists convention with ice cream soda

down the lost river in impractical trunks

in honeycomb tunnels a black market for tripe

a pillowcase stuffed with Post-it notes

documents the fall of an empire

a strawberry as a treat on Fridays

I surprised her in the service lift

in the winter palace touching base with Gerry

all around the retractable bollard

in rollerblades my lady rides

outside the faith school with cheese and onion

a hare bolts through the haberdashery department

at the Black Lodge with an all-day breakfast

a hash brown pricked with a golden fork

an evening alone with Simon Le Bon
body butter and the emergency flannel
a melted waxwork of Francis Pym

dappled shadows of jewels underfoot
in the foliage near the giant screen
the distant call of pre-recorded birds

a fox amongst the overcoats
a viper in an abandoned rucksack
in Darlington where the daisies prosper

I love the unpredictability of mushrooms
hissing goose in the innovation workshop
thrice around the skip my true love walks

baleful blue star shattered and mullioned
his ex-line manager a fabled beauty
Take On Me by A-Ha here on Silk

like everyone else I drink bottled water
sorting the butterscotch battering the waffles
in every painting a tiny thimble

the juice of three oranges handcrafted to order
an outcrop viewed from the House of Lords
an artisan sandwich for Coeur de Lion

a cruel wind distresses Giorgio Moroder
silver fish in silver rivers
this poultice made with itinerant labour

on the wild moors the yogurt coated peanuts
where warlock and cocksman Peter Cetera
bent over and wept for the glory of love

cosmic dust on occasional tables

rind smoulders clearly on CCTV

in the orange grove a fictional monk

on the low wall a deceptive apple

six bats hang from a solid spruce mug tree

the rhinestoned lunchbox of Ming the Merciless

a low blow in the model village

adverse camber at the Sea Life Centre

a new shoe for a basking shark

down the branch line in an on trend snood

oxeye daisies in the shadow of the health club

here the wands and quadrants are made

a canary is not a friend for life

a bent bough makes a poor companion

temporary lights on the shoulder of Orion

beyond the ridge a phalanx of fruiterers

I raised a level one grievance with Andrea

in a dingle on the road to Rotherham

celebration cakes and heritage sparklers

magnetic rail through the vale of Mordor

beneath the redoubt the bones of Mr Kipling

the shellac nails of the lady of the lake

the threaded brows of Morgan le Fay

in a bungalow with a vanquished elf

thrice betrayed in Randy's lounge

ensnared by fire in Newton-le-Willows

no mercy in the kingdom of Haribo

corduroy and instant noodles

coy mistress of late with your roaming limbs

up on the cliff top at a wizard's picnic

I loved her like a mulberry bush

I loved her like ideas in Rochdale

I loved her like a guinea pig

moonlight falls on imminent compost

in the Portakabin near the petrified city

they are plotting a putsch with pie and peas

something snapped during *Alvin and the Chipmunks*

there is Chinese writing on some of the awnings

there is lemongrass on the bowling green

in a dream he gave me chicken dippers

Nick Clegg plays pinball at a drop in centre

on clement evenings with an Epson printer

don't waste your energy on the wrong tariff

I want something easily eatable on my sofa

in the mountains where the snow falls all winter

balustrades and coloured panels

a rift in time near the anchovies

glowing after a night of fun

rain and every drop of silver

her long face and interminable autumn

at the open day with a skinny mocha

the chatter of apes in a carpeted cellar

like a dog he sickens without meat

pressed tongue and then pastrami on a shovel

slow day in the imaginary town

maze of elm and a ruckus in the brambles

the Lord Mayor wears a different lanyard

dead for a ducat in the air conditioned meadow

maidens how they rise unbidden from the tussocks

to dip marshmallows in the chocolate fountain

I gave him the slip outside the soap works

a jay perched on the information desk

a new dimension for luncheon meat

imagine this in Richmond upon Thames
imagine this in Bath or Mortlake
at Oxenholme the mezze platters

a sand storm on the traffic island
such delicacy the way they eat the crab sticks
I've been disappointed in China for years

a magical ringtone summons the hornets
twenty-eight of twenty-nine parents attended
they put Viagra in the Ovaltine

sword play in the breakout session
planking with the Marquis of Salisbury
a statement mirror in an unloved alcove

I boxed things off with Lisa Lever
illuminated fitfully by meteors
an apparition at the garden centre

what complaisance such bosky trees
all along the hops with Robin Locksley
in the dungeon where the sheriff keeps his quinoa

blue paint indicates the affected nostril

we used the fruit cocktail to create a diversion

our muffins are always English muffins

I get my kicks from *Coarse Fishing Monthly*

ham and cheese panini described in mime

inside each egg a tiny lozenge

combing over a cloth or towel

applying with gusto on the royal yacht

wild boar loose in the drumming workshop

hard times at the enchanted fortress

living on rain and Cup a Soup

six blown tins afloat in the storm drain

at the depot the mounds of malt loaf

hidden wiring chased with ebony

a message of support down the speaking tube

an improvised shoeshine the revolving doors

when they drop a cape and release the swans

when they open the vaults and coat the nuts

desolate in jodhpurs and barley gluten

dissociated at the sportsman's dinner

a bee and a tub of minibites

I won my colleagues over with gelatine

corned beef pie and a skillet of hake

black rain above the birding hide

I often spoil my wife with squid

ice and then the vegetable oil

till late in an armchair with Timothy Claypole

getting big laughs at the plenary

child friendly cordial and daddy's special flakes

when he wants it he lurks by the microwave

frisky at the craft beer tasting

organic mousse and astonishing lobster

a manifesto written in glitter glue

I dream of opening a hostel for rabbits

guerrilla perfumery in the former Yugoslavia

motivational signage at the monastery

back at the ranch for a peer review
a collection of antique drinking straws
for his fealty a tribute of almond milk

withdraw to the north and a fortress of rain
a siege economy of crispy pancakes
sausage casserole and early dark

I cherish the crumbs of my erstwhile mistress
her face in profile at the salad bar
at the sneeze guard where the ravens gather

party time in the client state

fun and games and the all-important pelvis

at the radar station in jellyfish season

I claim no knowledge of the territory

her moods and 95% humidity

upstream where they train the wolves

a roundhouse linked to a second roundhouse

a steady hand amongst the macaroons

we raised our standard in the horseradish

out on the hillocks the wandering rams

withdrawing a distant and sequestered turret

her magical raven needs new batteries

the wooded crags and bicycle sheds

the cattle and the tropical fish

the lavender and bends in the river

she pours the soup in a goblet for me

she puts the prawns in a jug for me

it is paradise here in Oak Furniture Land

the secret sonnets of Sabrina Salerno

she owns the river on Derby Road

in Bosnia on a croquet lawn

a brace of newly forgotten mackerel

in a grotto by the media centre

in a modern single storey dwelling

outside the circle the somnolent clams

wet lettuce where the monolith is

life is better with an empty bladder

an orchiectomy for Peter André
in cover afforded by purple foxgloves
welcoming careful drivers to Whitby

long white sky and long white cloud
reflected glass in glass reflected
a quiet booth with a nun or two

behind the waterfall a secret room
in the secret room in a secret drawer
a partial denture partially redacted

cast adrift with cream of coconut
beyond the ridge the coddled lychees
pudding rice steams in subterranean caverns

her serpentine and sonorous windpipe
at the lentil farm with a tightened buttock
struck dumb with wonder at the thermostat

cross hatched in the People's Republic
whilst thinking about Iranians or Persians
a chocolate brioche for bad King John

chunky marmalade in ancient pasture

water cress logjam where the capsule is

shepherds oiled up for a noble cause

begin by enumerating the pears

bent flange and an extra elbow

in the lock up garage with the Huguenots

rusty crowns in community gardens

why was Boromir chosen for the quest

who will be TV's next big cheese

doomed to failure at the bottle bank

is it you who puts the plastic bags in bushes

they melted the staples to make a broadsword

dog rose and bindweed a modest trove

toffee latte and a knotted pipe

Prince Charles leans on authentic hawthorn

the end of history in meeting room 11

like a wave or a sun blushed olive

a burnished apple for an action point

in some pictures I have no earlobes

another version an improvised world

like when they drink tea in the street on adverts

I was a musketeer a lollipop colourist

a doomed greengrocer the inventor of tinsel

I was a registered psychotherapist in Islington

slow snow at the summit a surprising lunchbox

walnut polish and the eye of Sauron

a soft-boiled egg will not fool anyone

there are golden goblets in the privet

there are longships on the boating lake

I filled a yogurt pot with foaming rain

I lost the ring on the upper deck

like a proud horse through the baby change

pale shadow on the oven housing

when it was written it was written on vellum

on a menu in the gated village

golden moon above the contemplation zone

long nights in the termite mound
broken biscuits in a tortoise shell chamber
stiff peel in the royal quarters

sexy like the lady at the loss adjustors
sexy like the vicar from *Gogglebox*
sexy like an artichoke

abandoned and raised by a family of bees
a linen suit for Kim Jong-un
a sensible shoe for a whimsical empress

in drizzle glass and gleaming cube
muted goldfish in tranquil pools
cool breeze by the llama factory

another morning in the eighteenth century
clavichords and gentleman's relish
damp elms bend at the edge of the acres

out on the moors the indomitable weasels
Graeme is in a car and cannot respond
prison hulks bob in the bay with lemon

all wrapped up in Merthyr Tydfil

sea green shake and last minute buns

down the culvert in a rudimentary coracle

dough balls at the business park

she bought me a crumpet and showed me Weatherfield

the fall of Rome from Frankie and Benny's

in a previous life I made a fresco

a tonsure and impacted molars

they mix up the oxtail in a special vessel

drunk at the ice rink on ginger wine

they are breaded now the bearded clams

cheesy chips and a cheeky apple

on the giant inflatable the Russian oligarchs

osprey eggs and hi-gloss cream

a watch struck dumb in a waistcoat pocket

cookies and caramel praline swansdown

I hired the tools from a gentleman farmer

bent spoons to pull the jelly from the creels

plaintive greengage a burgundy fern

a lucrative seam of porridge oats

no ponies in the parmesan mines

I've just finished *The Shock of the Fall*

I've just finished *The Casual Vacancy*

I've just finished *The History of Salami*

I built a home for terrapins with him

I balanced a brick on a shoebox with him

sudden asparagus amongst the putty

sky blue Vitara an ermine cagoule

three terriers named after Soviet communists

this face is made from coloured rice

my wife cooks meatballs while I make a spreadsheet

I burnt my thumb on the rim of the roast

I ate the mustard straight from the spoon

I like fireworks but not those fireworks

I like poodles but not those poodles

I like cheese scones but they make me fat

blue stars blaze on the handball court
pack ice and her frozen shoulder
guttering lamps on the roller rink

I took advice at the pelvic workshop
I got strong armed by a haberdasher
I thought of a use for some random nuts

at certain points the slabs are misaligned
like a free PDF from a qualified life coach
like a blank look from an itinerant falconer

winter nights in the tilted room
her face on one side her face on the other
crispy pancakes in the pressure cooker

what to do with all this ornament
we are living in a time of sweet chilli flakes
we are living in a time of anchovies

I unlocked an achievement at the walk-in centre
I unlocked an achievement at Tesco Extra
I got a badge and I'm dolphin friendly

giant pandas are just men in suits
giant Schnauzers are just men in suits
giant poodles are just men in suits

there is no such thing as thundersnow
there is no such thing as instant trifle
there is no such thing as the lumbar spine

here in the north we make our own fish
we can make mist and raspberry foam
we can make fire with tempura vegetables

morning moon and yellow goose

she gets up early to polish the eggs

she rubs me down with a vintage text gauntlet

molten cheese and Just For Men

I wear a checked shirt to work sometimes

I had an accident and it wasn't my fault

I did my gap year in Grange-over-Sands

I wrote a novel about aromatherapy

I tried it all from lip gloss to latte

Monday morning cheese string and mustard
bare knuckle fight with a digital eagle
abroad in willow wood with inconstant hound

beef paté on a pointless Tuesday
I blocked the only exit from the lounge
I troubled a warlock with niceties

chips and dips in the court of King Zog
head for the shrubbery and triangulate there
a sequinned cod piece is animal magic

cheese moments in the magic hollow

by the weeping willow a measure of relish

the silver grass strewn with golden breadcrumbs

.

wadded tissue in a Raglan sleeve

love and being loved in Ashton-under-Lyne

a wanker's charter for Bertram Muffet

black listed at the sushi bar

banned for life from the wetlands centre

into exile in a Nissan Micra

bumptious in pumps and sleeveless jerkin

isolated at the AGM

crystal clear in Wetherspoons

I discovered poetry in 1887

I just got fat on the rail replacement bus

I split the difference with Joanne Thunder

somewhere in the sustainable forest

a strongbox full of pulverised parsley

under stress I sometimes handle the rubbings

cracked jewel hair curtain white winter face
pale and cloudburst muffled birdsong
over there by the fax machine

there are yellow books but I haven't read them
barking fox in the lunar module
undercut by bathos in the rhubarb patch

she lays her perfect head on the sideboard
I entertain her with my phantom finger
we raise our flags where the squirrels live

candied peel in the bivouac

the hams laid out and lavender

itemised passions and Lucozade Sport

stranded at the bake off branded a fool

all along the gangplank the heritage plaques

big Jim rings the devil's doorbell

white funk like a dog on wheels

they didn't do this at Studio 54

slowly with an addled milk shake

look there are no nettles here
in a stranglehold with a tame koala
in a tracksuit with a cucumber portion

set the controls to maximum cherry
sundown over the smoking shelter
lost hope on the shuttle bus

there are blue lights on the rim of the universe
roundabout route through the badminton community
a metaphor for a chastised goatherd

got momentum and a bunch of grapes
sugar rush for a period beatnik
that feeling you get at the rodeo

almost everyone has had a little tingle
almost everyone has been in a ditch
almost everyone has ice boots now

hysteria at the bowling green
the swooping birds and then the weasels
if you can't breathe the oxygen listen to Toto

the sadness of empty plastic bottles
the sadness of fungus the sorrow of canaries
I seem of late to have lost my mirth

Viennese coffee and yellow ringlets
something now is making it weird
Hall & Oates on predictive text

I saw her alone in the rockery
I saw her riding a llama indefinitely
next week she'll be wearing my rollneck

banana breakfast fluoxetine on toast
unhurried intimacy in the arboretum
broken fractals star syntax biscuits

someone should have shaved more carefully
someone should have held down the butter
someone gave me poisoned seaweed

they have nailed the cheese strings to the branches
I'm going Dutch this basketball season
a mortal blow from Diego Simeone

special egg for a special day
the dried peas hidden beneath the bracken
sudden loss of nerve in the scullery

the I Ching told me to go back on Facebook
magical coins a rune on the forearm
glowing stones on a rainy Sabbath

they did a sketch and sealed the premises
they destroyed the paté with a wanton gesture
if your pots are missing try the box by the cork board

out in the amber precincts with Robinson

a signal conveyed by the medium of muesli

the ill-advised musculature of molluscs

lightly salted by a forest ranger

slumped in silence at the siege of Orleans

ensnared in the eaves by a lure of lemons

she holds a mirror tilted inwards

she roams unhindered through the National Parks

between the cairns with a modicum of cheddar

flat belly meal in salt awareness week

octopus fingers in the freezer section

sensual salad and the wonders of mustard

sidereal motion in the Portakabin

six stars occluded by hanging baskets

seven stars dried in a plastic bucket

out on a limb with the orthopaedic surgeons

lashed to the mast on the Norfolk Broads

I could catch a bus and be home tomorrow

things feel better when you have a plan
fajitas burgers steaks wraps nachos
no equilibrium in the Wacky Warehouse

pumped up on the bouncy castle
absolutely buzzing at the Buddhist retreat
high on life with the Scottish Widows

protein shake in the mindfulness session
mallow grass on a managed desktop
blond sun sheen on plains of formica

to the cute guy in the faux leather jacket

to Lynne from Glasgow where the porridge is

I am the Afro-haired girl you speak of

to the cute blonde on Wednesday at Ruislip Gardens

to the lady from Orpington where there are no coconuts

I am the small brunette in gym gear

got myself bright yellow briefcase

got myself a brand new tripod

in a car on the soft verge with Level 42

bewildered by birds and obscured clouds
salted caramels and the rain charms of Watford
no Shetland ponies in the land of the giants

I thrashed out a methodology with Roberto
he substituted me in the second leg
he burst my bubble in his caravan

deep assignment in herbaceous borders
a sacred spoon on the equinox
compartment syndrome on the road to ruin

little capsules half yellow half white
tincture of stinkhorn syrup of figs
strong as a salmon in a pastry basket

lean asparagus and body butter
I looked askance while he measured the melons
I watched on helpless as he sculpted a radish

bad boys in honey and liposuction
a flourishing trade in elderberries
a body crisis for the Duke of Anjou

in the foyer ghosts of Beefeaters
glowing snow globes of itinerant Martians
petals drift down meandering conduits

the vicar mounts occasional tables
his wife and her world of underwater knowledge
there the clinkers and there the embers

self-portrait with a twisted lanyard
someone forgot to mince the onions
someone forgot to cancel the gammon

no quarter given at the numeracy workshop

carefully navigating a Japanese restaurant

weight of a dumpling in an inside pocket

twist of citrus a column of elves

they put the peelings in a pillow case

they shaved the dogs and put them on YouTube

further abroad in a scarlet tunic

I made an effort and opened a window

I gave short shrift to his wobbly whistle

the incandescent rage of captured beavers
the crumpled bells of Berkhamstead abbey
I can't be around uncomplicated people

the river and the river repeats itself
smoked paprika in a lime tree arbour
the spirit and flesh in Shrewsbury is weak

I thought of her there effaced by pylons
I sympathised as he pulled on the waders
if you could bottle it I'd eat it with sweetcorn

I'm done with it now the crooked pillars
brown rice seaweed dirty hot dog
I saw Colonel Sanders in an opium haze

we shared an arm rest as far as Crewe
nice and shy in a farmhouse together
lack of chemistry at East Midlands Parkway

they pile up the earth and ruin on ruin
they make the daffodils out of Lego
no lyric impulse at Bristol Temple Meads

refried beans and emotional sincerity

blue moon yellow moon empty window

air of solemnity at the leaflet library

love in the time of apple blossom

love in the time of silver rain

love on the gravel where the rabbits are

frozen shoulder on the ides of March

hysteria in the golden section

in a dream I was a content manager

an intimate brunch with the Marquis de Sade

a walk in the park with Murun Buchstansangur

a hansom cab shared with Taylor Swift

a secret technique for mandarin segments

inflatable friends and holiday spam

chillaxing in Bognor with Banquo's ghost

hands free in the monastery garden

they made amends with cottage cheese

a boarded loft is no place for rollerball

soy and ginger magic noodles
rubber dolphin corrugated beeswax
these things I bring as tokens of peace

she puts her velvet curtains on eBay
she drops the toast and is devil may care
black light falls on the *Countdown* conundrum

smelting ore with a long lost uncle
he's got this gift with fire extinguishers
during earthquakes he finds an auxiliary lever

vodka gold dust with Farrant and Kroch

cold fish supper and lumpy doughnuts

down in the bunker where Don Revie lives

years pass and are empty of wonders

the white dog walks through the afternoon

slow snow falls in the Bailiwick of Guernsey

a bow tie and a flying jacket

royal jelly in a Thermos flask

a kiwi cares but little for brittle

a dream result for lovers of cheese

Balfour Beatty beef briquette

our martyrs are always English martyrs

occult vibrations at Namco Funscape

Rainbow Brite and Strawberry Shortcake

a single spark from a discrete unit

I put the peas in a pressurised cabin

don't let heartburn ruin your honeymoon

after eight in a closed car with Justin Bieber

a spiral staircase obscured by clouds
damask rose and Hampton in duck egg
drones overhead in the court of Adolphus

here the miniature potters came ashore
their trembling hands their intricate glaze
England there in the folds of rain

I touched my smart card near the ant hill
I stole a marrow from my lady's cold frame
her gaze across the darkening river

curious orb and darkening steeple
oily fish on days of obligation
soft cheese pillows the treachery of eels

the lack of an overarching idea
the universe alone and fragments
feeling the burn with a Russian oligarch

I romped through the heather as a random gesture
I put the pudding where the slats overlapped
I dropped a bombshell in the nunnery

the apparition of those faces in the crowd

Yankee candles Lizard Lick Towing

empty room and spider under glass

red bricks and the orange bricks

mid-table finish for Septimus Severus

sticklebacks flicker in a gloomy ditch

eat fresh until 11th May

in two and three-bedroom quality apartments

freshly cut in Chipping Sodbury

tiny blonde with sparkly blue eyes
I passed out on the 8:11 train
my rabbit loves his outdoor hutch

badly let down by a wandering minstrel
formerly one of the greatest axemen
a petit pain for Anne Boleyn

the bins concealed by a rustic dwelling
just five minutes from junction 11
the skulls of kings and hollyhocks and bees

the girl downstairs with awesome sourdough

corn rows and a vacant pocket

eighteen holes with the prince of Bohemia

around this time I invented the doily

supple in gabardine a golden blown trumpet

a picture of Rotterdam a tumbled oak

solar panels on the royal igloo

lost in a labyrinth of watercress and rocket

at the farmers' market encumbered by mittens

auto immune in a smoking jacket

at the manse with jelly and laudanum

one rook does not a rookery make

like an alligator in World of Leather

like a Shih Tzu trapped in a plastic bucket

like a snake disguised as a smaller snake

when they put the squeeze on Simon & Garfunkel

in a seminar on spontaneous improvement

across with ocean with a burst baguette

lily livered sad eyed boys

Ferrero Rocher and milk of magnesia

no birds in the underground feasting hall

deep pan crustless golden mead

lilacs and a boneless bucket

her velveteen skin her incurious lips

the aimless erudition of astronauts

a strand of this and a strand of that

knotted limbs in the cool down session

Venus and Mars and latterly Mercury
crème de cacao crème de menthe
magical moments for everyday Britons

thank you Tracy for finding my oyster
the swaying masts of the business park
an incantation for a makeshift barrier

a story about chocolate with seven flavours
unlimited hog roast sunrise to sunset
a pulled pork salad for the Ancient Mariner

photobombed by John of Gaunt

above the ruins of Weston-super-Mare

effortless waves at the Recipe Cottage

a complete shambles at the model village

an influence on clothes and shoulder pads

mushroom stroganoff in a nuanced context

a hero overcoming punctuation

a diagram of planned canals

Einstein at the beach with perfect abs

local chutney cashback salad bowl
a single word commands the hornets
minestrone flashbacks in clogs and poncho

I loved and lost with resistant glass
I followed her into the mini-mart
behind the ears the essence of Kong

is it you who brought the liquorice torpedoes
is if you who signed off the halibut
in the bottom drawer a breaded fritter

led astray in a monogrammed kimono
re-united after losing four stone
the tanning salons of unreal cities

all alone in the glove compartment
unquiet spirits of the haunted wardrobe
ectoplasm in plastic beakers

food to go and seaweed peanuts
sugared almonds the curve of her shoulder
all the brave sublunary things

Printed in Great Britain
by Amazon